She
Persisted

....

MARGARET
CHASE SMITH

....

— INSPIRED BY —

She Persisted

by Chelsea Clinton & Alexandra Boiger

MARGARET CHASE SMITH

Written by
Ruby Shamir

Interior illustrations by
Gillian Flint

PHILOMEL

PHILOMEL BOOKS
An imprint of Penguin Random House LLC, New York

First published in the United States of America by Philomel Books,
an imprint of Penguin Random House LLC, 2021

Library of Congress Cataloging-in-Publication Data is available.

Manufactured in Italy

HC ISBN 9780593115893
10 9 8 7 6 5 4 3 2 1
PB ISBN 9780593115909
10 9 8 7 6 5 4 3 2 1

GV

Edited by Jill Santopolo.
Design by Ellice M. Lee.
Text set in LTC Kennerley.

⁓ In memory of ⁓
Safta Rachel, who persisted
through extreme adversity to build
a new life in her new country

She Persisted

DEAR READER,

As Sally Ride and Marian Wright Edelman both powerfully said, "You can't be what you can't see." When Sally Ride said that, she meant that it was hard to dream of being an astronaut, like she was, or a doctor or an athlete or anything at all if you didn't see someone like you who already had lived that dream. She especially was talking about seeing women in jobs that historically were held by men.

I wrote the first *She Persisted* and the books that came after it because I wanted young girls—and children of all genders—to see women who worked hard to live their dreams. And I wanted all of us to see examples of persistence in the face of different challenges to help inspire us in our own lives.

I'm so thrilled now to partner with a sisterhood of writers to bring longer, more in-depth versions of these stories of women's persistence and achievement to readers. I hope you enjoy these chapter books as much as I do and find them inspiring and empowering.

And remember: If anyone ever tells you no, if anyone ever says your voice isn't important or your dreams are too big, remember these women. They persisted and so should you.

Warmly,

Chelsea Clinton

MARGARET CHASE SMITH

TABLE OF CONTENTS

....

Reaching High on Tippy-Toes

When Margaret Chase was a little girl, no one would have thought to ask what she wanted to be when she grew up. In those days, it didn't much matter what a girl *wanted* to be, because there were very real limits on what she *could* be. She was supposed to get married to a man and be a mother. And if she had to work outside the home to make money, there were very few jobs for which she would be hired—maybe a maid or a teacher or a waitress or a store clerk. Women weren't expected to be much else, and more than that, they weren't supposed to *want* much else. Women weren't expected to have ambition—goals or dreams that they could work hard to make happen.

But from the start, Margaret had ambition: she wanted to build her own future in her own way.

Margaret was born on December 14, 1897, and grew up in the mill town of Skowhegan, Maine, a largely white community, where many people worked in the factories along the Kennebec River. Her father was a barber and her mother was a waitress and a store clerk, and washed other people's laundry. Her family worked hard for everything they had, which included a horse, a pig, a cow, and some chickens. They grew vegetables in their garden and had window boxes filled with flowers in the spring.

The oldest of six kids, Margaret became her mother's partner in taking care of the house and the other children. Margaret didn't mind. She loved and admired her mother and she loved to work, especially once she figured out that hard work was the key to a different kind of future. "I went to work because I wanted to be independent," she said. "I wanted to spend my own money as I wanted to. And I did. That is exactly what I did."

When Margaret was twelve, she tried to get a job at a small store in town, but she couldn't reach the merchandise on the high shelf behind the counter. The shop owner joked that she should

apply for the job later when she was taller. But it wasn't a joke to Margaret. She was serious about working there, and once she was thirteen years old, she finally was tall enough to reach the top shelf standing on her tippy-toes. She got the job.

It was the first of many jobs Margaret would have. She was a quick learner and a hard worker and always impressed her bosses.

While she was in high school, she got her second job, as a telephone operator. In the early 1900s, long before anyone had a cell phone, few people even had telephones in their homes, but those who did couldn't call each other directly. To reach someone by telephone, callers would first have to phone a switchboard operator. The operator would then connect callers to whomever they wanted to talk to. For this job, Margaret had to memorize the telephone directory and learn the technical skills to connect the calls, chatting with the callers all the while. The work put her at the center of what was happening in town and showed her how the people in her community were linked to one another. She also found she could be a helper, connecting people to doctors, firefighters, and police officers during emergencies.

It was through this work that, at age sixteen, she met Clyde Smith, a well-known and well-liked businessman who was more than twenty years older than her. He had run as a candidate for some local elections and won. As Skowhegan's first selectman, which was a bit like being the mayor, he ran town meetings and oversaw a lot of town business. When Margaret was seventeen, Clyde

offered her a job in his office keeping and updating important records for the town. She got her first real taste of politics and public service, helping him help others and learning from him.

Margaret liked high school and enjoyed playing for the championship girls' basketball team, but she loved her work best—it gave her a sense of freedom and her own money so she didn't have to depend on anyone else. It was through her work that she could stretch herself, on her tippy-toes if she had to, and reach heights she hadn't yet even imagined.

CHAPTER 2

Leaping into the Future

By the time Margaret graduated from high school in 1916, women's roles and opportunities were starting to change a bit. Women did not yet have the right to vote, but they were actively fighting for it, and more young women began working in more types of jobs. Even fashion changed—women began to cut their hair shorter, dress in skirts that rose above their ankles, and wear lipstick. Margaret took part in those changes.

As more women worked in professional jobs, they began to meet and talk about how to be more successful in their careers. Margaret soon joined them at the Business and Professional Women's Clubs, also called the BPW. In the BPW, she met women like her, women who had ambition. She was well-liked and good at getting things done, but most of all she worked hard and had an independent spirit—she did things her own way—which other women in the BPW admired.

Margaret also discovered that she was a leader. She became president of the BPW of Maine when she was twenty-seven. At the time, she was the youngest woman to reach that position. She also continued to be a superb worker in job after job: at the telephone company, and later at the weekly newspaper, and after that at a really tough job

where she was in charge of much more experi-
enced workers at a wool mill. She even ran for local
office, to be a member of the Skowhegan Town
Committee, and won reelection twice. She didn't

know very much about politics, she later said, "but I knew everybody and everybody knew me. It was just a natural thing. Call it destiny if you will, but I just fell into it."

Margaret married Clyde Smith in May 1930, as he continued to rise in politics. After running for election for different jobs in his town and in the state, Clyde decided to run for a seat in the House of Representatives, which would bring him to Washington, DC, if he won.

The United States Congress is divided into two parts, called chambers: the House of Representatives and the Senate. Members of the House are elected to represent their districts, which are sections of their state. They have to run for reelection every two years. Members of the Senate serve for six-year terms and represent their whole state in Congress, not just a small slice of it. Together, the House of Representatives and the Senate vote to make the laws for the whole country. The President of the United States signs those laws and makes sure they are carried out.

Candidates, the people hoping to win elections for those and other roles in government, speak to audiences, shake hands, kiss babies, pose for photos, and attend dinners and luncheons with members of the public. How do all those meetings and events translate into votes on Election Day? It isn't magic. It takes hard work by the candidate and the people who are working to elect the candidate, work that those crowds might not see or notice.

Margaret was in charge of all of that background work for Clyde's 1936 race for the House of Representatives. She marked his every move on a hand-drawn map of the district, so he'd remember where he had visited. She wrote letters to every person he met and created files of issues that mattered to them so that Clyde could keep his promises to help them. Like many candidates, Clyde made speeches during the campaign, which were exciting in the moment. But candidates need to follow through on what they say in those speeches so that voters trust and support them. Margaret was a master at that work.

After Clyde won the election, he wanted Margaret to continue helping him in Washington, DC. She agreed on one condition: that he pay her a salary. She understood her value, and knew that getting paid for her work showed the world that she should be taken seriously.

As Clyde became very ill during his time in

Congress, he needed Margaret's help even more.
She kept the office running and traveled to meetings and events in his place. One evening in the
spring of 1940, after giving a big speech for him in

Maine, Margaret got an urgent message: She had to rush back home to Washington, DC, because her husband's illness had suddenly gotten worse. He was dying.

In the days that followed, Clyde sent a message to the voters of his community: if he could no longer campaign, they should vote for Margaret. "I know of no one who has the full knowledge of my ideas and plans or is as well qualified as she is, to carry on these ideas and my unfinished work for the district." Clyde died the next day.

Margaret was motivated to do all that unfinished work, this time out front, not just in the background. As a modern working woman, she was ready to leap into the future. She just had to convince the voters of Skowhegan to give her a chance.

CHAPTER 3

Running on Her Own

Margaret did not have much time to mourn her husband's passing. On the day of Clyde's funeral, several other people began their campaigns against her for his former House seat. In June 1940, she had to win a special election to take Clyde's seat in Congress for the rest of the term he had been elected for, and then she had to run in another election in the fall for a full two-year term of her own.

Races for Congress are never easy, but these races were especially challenging for a simple reason: Margaret was a woman, and there weren't many women who had been elected for any position, anywhere. Margaret's experience with politics was rare for a woman. You could count on your fingers the number of women in all of the United States Congress at that time.

Up until twenty years earlier, women hadn't even been allowed to vote. By the time Margaret was running in her election, many voters—men and women alike—still weren't sure if women could be trusted to make important laws and decisions, like whether or not the country should go to war. Some of Margaret's opponents said being a Member of Congress "is a man's job." Voters liked her, they believed she could do a good job, but some of them weren't quite sure a woman should have power, and she certainly shouldn't *want* it. Margaret brushed off those concerns and kept her campaign message simple: she wanted to be elected so she could help people. She said, "Vote for the one who will vote for you."

Margaret won the seat on Election Day. And she won every time she ran for reelection over the next six years. During those years, she traveled every inch of her district and remembered the names and personal details of the people she met. Then she went back to Washington to speak out for their concerns. She answered every letter she got. All this hard work showed the people of her district what they knew in their hearts when they had voted for her: that being a woman

made no difference, and that she could do a great job for them because she cared, plain and simple.

Margaret didn't do only what was expected of her, she did more. She supported equal rights for women, a courageous stand to take at the time. She snuck into a jail to study the awful conditions of the women and girls who were being held there. She pushed for the government to help working mothers with childcare. She visited with troops serving in a war in Saipan, an island in the Pacific Ocean, where she had to run from gunshots. She came back home an even bigger champion of America's soldiers. Margaret was a sensation.

On a congressional trip to Europe and the Middle East, she addressed the governments in England and Iran, and handed out lollipops to children she saw on the streets. On the flight back to the United States, a few of the engines on the plane broke down. Margaret remained calm, passing around harmonicas she had bought in Switzerland and leading the other passengers

in song. The plane landed safely, though it was a difficult flight. "I was just as scared as the rest of them," she said later on. "Only as a woman I couldn't have the luxury of showing my fear."

After seven years serving in the House of Representatives, Margaret had become hugely popular in Maine. She was so good at helping her constituents, the people who lived in her district, that Mainers who lived outside of her district asked for her help too. Why not try for the job representing all Mainers in Congress? Why not run for the US Senate? Margaret was the best qualified and the hardest working of all the politicians in the state.

One reason not to was that no woman in American history had ever served in both chambers of Congress, in the House and then in the

Senate. But Margaret never held herself back just because something had not been done before. Ever independent in thought and spirit, she imagined a future she could build for herself and paved a path forward.

·····························

CHAPTER 4

Speaking Up Courageously

Margaret ran for the United States Senate the same way that she had always run for office. She traveled all over the state, listened to people, and explained to them that just as she had served the people of her district, she could help all the people of Maine.

Margaret inspired an army of volunteers who were passionate about her. One teenage girl sent her a dollar for the campaign and wrote, "I regret only two things: that this must be merely a token contribution to your senatorial campaign and that I am not yet old enough to vote."

Almost two out of every three voters in Maine were women and Margaret asked for their votes, not because she was a woman, but because of her record in Congress helping the people of her district. Women's organizations, like the BPW she had led years before, supported Margaret. When her opponents said that the Senate was "no place for a woman," Margaret responded that that was "a direct challenge to every woman in Maine." And she was right. She won a huge victory, getting more votes than all three of her opponents combined.

After an election, each senator must take an oath of office, promising to defend the United

States Constitution, which is what American laws are based on. When Margaret was sworn in as senator in January 1949, women traveled from all

around the country to celebrate her win. Then, pinning a fresh rose to the top of her dress each day, Margaret got to work.

Eyes everywhere were on Margaret, which was bad and good. It was bad because she got attention for things that didn't matter to her job—what outfit she was wearing or what her favorite recipes were. It was good because it meant people paid attention to her work passing laws and improving her state.

Early on, she faced a big challenge. There was a famous Republican senator, Joseph McCarthy, who accused innocent people of being traitors to America. He tried to get them jailed or fired from their jobs. No one was standing up to him because they were afraid he would call them traitors too.

Margaret thought McCarthy's behavior was

shameful. She refused to stay quiet about his bullying. Even though she was new to the Senate, she decided to give a major speech about why McCarthy's actions were wrong.

On June 1, 1950, she was heading from her office to the floor of the Senate, the Senate's big meeting hall, when she ran into McCarthy.

"Margaret," he said. "You look very serious. Are you going to make a speech?"

"Yes," she replied. "And you will not like it."

Margaret was brave, even though she was also nervous. That's usually how courage works—you need it most when you are the most scared. McCarthy sat two rows behind her during her speech. Margaret began speaking in a shaky voice.

"I speak as a Republican. I speak as a woman. I speak as a United States senator. I speak as an

American." Then she went on to remind her
fellow senators that it was their job to protect
Americans' rights and freedoms. Even though she
didn't mention McCarthy's name, she went after
his bullying.

She said, "Those of us who shout the loudest

about Americanism . . . are all too frequently those who, by our own words and acts, ignore some of the basic principles of Americanism—the right to criticize. The right to hold unpopular beliefs. The right to protest. The right of independent thought."

Independent thought—the ability to have your own beliefs and make your own decisions—was something Margaret cared about not only for herself, but for all Americans. And while some people agreed with her and called her speech "magnificent" and "noble," others criticized it as "selfish" and "harmful." But whatever people thought of it, the speech made it clear that Margaret was brave and independent, and willing to act and speak up against wrongdoing. One well-known leader at the time said that if a man had given that speech, he would be the next president of the United States.

Margaret was a first-term senator, and becoming president was not on her mind. Not yet, anyway. She had too much other work to do.

....

CHAPTER 5

Working Extra Hard

F or Margaret, there was no such thing as spare time. She filled every moment she had with work. As an elected official, she took very seriously her job to serve the public. She would never let the people of Maine down.

As the first and only woman at the time to do many things, Margaret had to be extra prepared, extra brave, and extra perfect because she was watched extra closely. It was a big responsibility.

When she first started in the Senate, men would stand whenever she walked into the room, believing this was how they needed to behave around a lady. She didn't want to be treated differently, but she also didn't want to embarrass the men by telling them to stop. So she found a solution that meant she ended up working a little harder than anyone else. She showed up extra early to meetings, so she'd already be there sitting in her seat when the men arrived and they wouldn't feel pressured to stand up for her.

It was the same way she faced every challenge. Margaret became the first woman senator in American history to lead a big investigation that was broadcast on television after she learned that US soldiers fighting in Korea didn't have the supplies they needed. At first, the military leaders treated Margaret "like a lady who didn't know anything, gave me a pat on the head." But she persisted, and often asked the tough questions that other, male senators wouldn't ask. She even lifted her chair on wooden blocks so that the men wouldn't seem taller than her. One person who

worked with her said the military leaders eventually took her seriously "because she demanded they did. That didn't mean that they liked her, but they developed respect for her and the way she did her job."

As time went on, more and more people appreciated her leadership. She hosted President Dwight Eisenhower for a cookout in her backyard in Skowhegan, Maine. He broiled his own steak and Margaret found a way to supply over one hundred reporters traveling with him with delicious Maine lobsters. She debated the former first lady Eleanor Roosevelt on television about the 1956 presidential election. She was the first woman in Congress to break the sound barrier, which meant flying at almost one thousand miles per hour, during an air force training session. In part because of her firm support in Congress of the space program, America launched astronauts to the moon. She did all this while also serving in the US Air Force Reserve.

Throughout, she stayed closely connected to the people of Maine. She ran for reelection in 1954 and again in 1960, and she won both races by many votes. She also never lost her honorable and independent spirit. It was one of the reasons that she voted for the Civil Rights Act of 1960, which supported the rights of African Americans and did more to ensure that all Americans had an equal opportunity to vote.

As always, Margaret got a lot of mail. Now among the regular requests from Mainers for help were letters urging her to run for president against President John F. Kennedy in the 1964 election. In November of 1963, when President Kennedy was asked about Margaret, he said he "would not look forward" to running against her because she was "very formidable as a political figure." In other words, she'd be tough to beat.

President Kennedy was killed one week later. It was a tragedy that shocked and saddened the nation. Now was not the time to think about politics, and Margaret stopped answering questions about whether or not she would run for president.

President Kennedy had been a senator before he was elected president in 1960. Just before his funeral, Margaret walked to his old seat in the Senate, removed the rose that was pinned to her top, and left it on his desk. While Margaret had disagreed with President Kennedy on many issues, her action showed that on the most important matters, in the most difficult times, people could come

together as Americans. America should be a place, she believed, open to people who held different beliefs, people of independent thought, who could work together peacefully and respectfully for the common good.

·····························

CHAPTER 6

The First, Not the Last

A few months later, on January 27, 1964, Margaret spoke to an audience at the Women's National Press Club about reasons for and against running for president.

On the one hand, she had heard from supporters all over the country begging her to enter the race. On the other hand, she understood that Americans probably weren't ready to elect a woman president. Nonetheless, Margaret decided to try, and she would do it as she had done everything else in her life: in her own way.

The first contests of the presidential race would be primaries that moved from state to state, starting in New Hampshire in February of 1964. During primary contests, each party—the Democratic Party and the Republican Party— chose its candidate. Since Margaret was a Republican, she ran against other Republicans in the primary. If she won enough votes, she would be chosen as the Republican nominee for president, and would then run in the general election in November against whoever the Democrats had chosen.

Margaret opened her campaign for the Republican nomination in a tiny New Hampshire village called Pittsburg on a freezing-cold February morning—it was twenty-eight degrees below zero, cold enough to turn a soda into a slushy! She went door to door, visiting barbershops and post offices, diners and town halls, looking people in the eye and chatting with them. Over the next six days, she met ten thousand people and covered one thousand miles.

Margaret attracted a lot of adoring supporters. In a moment that was a reminder of her first
run for Senate, one ten-year old girl sent her a
dollar with a note that said, "This is my *own*
money that I saved for you." It could have been
young Margaret herself, determined to spend her
money as she wanted to.

Successful, modern presidential campaigns
depended on lots of money, lots of paid workers,
and lots of travel, but Margaret had never cam-
paigned that way before and she wasn't about to
change her winning formula. She wouldn't take
a penny for the campaign—she didn't want to
"owe" donors for her victories—so she returned
that dollar and other donations that came pouring
in. And she refused to miss any of her work in
the Senate. There was another, even bigger civil

rights bill up for debate. It would change the law so that African Americans couldn't be treated worse than white people—couldn't be discriminated against—and she did not want to miss the chance to vote for it.

This time, though, her campaign plan would not work. Margaret didn't win in New Hampshire and she didn't win the few other state contests where her name was on the ballot. She did, however, win enough votes to attend the Republican National Convention in California. According to tradition, candidates were not supposed to sit among the crowds at conventions during nominating time. But Margaret wanted to be there on this historic night.

Margaret wore a bright red dress and sat in a box overlooking the rowdy convention hall.

Her friend Senator George Aiken gave a speech as he nominated her. He said that Margaret had "courage to stand for the right when it may not be popular to do so—courage to stand for

decency in the conduct of public affairs—courage to stand alone if necessary against formidable odds."

At that moment, Margaret Chase Smith became the first woman in American history to be nominated for president by a major political party. The first, but not the last.

Today, ten times more women serve in Congress than when Margaret first got there. She paved the way for women to pursue their dreams of public service through all kinds of elected positions. Long after she retired to her home in Skowhegan, Maine, which is now the Margaret Chase Smith Library for congressional research, she said her life's work showed "that I was a woman and could do what a man could do without apologizing."

From the time she was a young girl, Margaret Chase Smith reached for the highest heights and did what she knew was right. She never stopped persisting—and neither should you.

HOW YOU CAN PERSIST

by Ruby Shamir

Margaret Chase Smith worked hard to achieve her dreams. Do you want to reach new heights in your life too? Here are some things you can do:

1. Stand up for anyone who is being bullied. Margaret made a difference by standing up to Joseph McCarthy's bullying.

2. Work hard. Margaret knew that working hard was the best way to make her dreams come true.

3. Study what you love. If you find a topic you are interested in, learn everything you can about it, like Margaret did about the military.

4. Support women's and girls' rights. Girls and women have the same right to do anything as boys and men. Spread the word!

5. Learn about leaders like Margaret. Visit the Margaret Chase Smith Library in Skowhegan, Maine, in person or online to learn more about her life and work.

6. Keep up the good work, win or lose. After Margaret lost the race for the

presidency, she stayed in the Senate for another eight years, serving the people of Maine.

7. Don't forget you have a voice. People didn't always want to listen to Margaret because she was a woman. People might think they shouldn't have to listen to you because you're a kid. They are wrong! You have important ideas to share at any age.

Acknowledgments

....

First, a big thank-you to Chelsea Clinton for writing about the extraordinary women featured in this series, women who widened the path forward for all of us who follow in their footsteps. Chelsea and Alexandra Boiger brought these persisters to life, giving them shape and texture in the gorgeous She Persisted picture books and giving young children access to their inspiring stories.

I'm so grateful to Chelsea for welcoming me into the Persisterhood, and to my editors, Jill Santopolo and Talia Benamy, for the precision and wisdom of their edits. Thanks to Gillian Flint for partnering on this book with her perfect illustrations. Thanks to the entire amazing team at Philomel: Ellice Lee for design, Shanta Newlin for promotion, Shara Hardeson for fact-checking, and Krista Ahlberg for copyediting. Thank you to my kind, caring, wise, incredibly skilled agent, Miriam Altshuler, for always having my back. Finally and always, thank you, Nick, Dante, Allegra, and Romy for your love and support.

⌐ References ⌐

Fitzpatrick, Ellen. "The Unfavored Daughter:
When Margaret Chase Smith Ran in the
New Hampshire Primary." *New Yorker*,
February 6, 2016.

Perlstein, Rick. "1964 Republican Convention:
Revolution From the Right," *Smithsonian
Magazine*, August 2008.

Senate Historical Office. "Mach-Buster Maggie: The Supersonic Senator from Maine." Senate. gov, December 3, 1957. https://www.senate .gov/artandhistory/history/minute/Mach _Buster_Maggie.htm.

Sherman, Janann. *No Place for a Woman: A Life of Senator Margaret Chase Smith*. New Brunswick, NJ: Rutgers University Press, 2001.

Smith, Margaret Chase. "Declaration of Conscience." Senate.gov, June 1, 1950. https:// www.senate.gov/artandhistory/history /resources/pdf/SmithDeclaration.pdf.

Wallace, Patricia Ward. *Politics of Conscience:*
A Biography of Margaret Chase Smith.
Westport, CT: Praeger, 1995.

RUBY SHAMIR is an award-winning children's book author whose titles include the What's the Big Deal About . . . American history and civics series, and *Bunny Figures It Out*. She previously worked in government and politics—in the White House, in the US Senate, and on a bunch of campaigns— and writes to share with readers what she learned about civic engagement in those roles. She lives in the Bronx, New York, with her husband and three children.

Photo credit: *Dafna Israel-Kotok*

You can visit Ruby Shamir online at
rubyshamir.com
or follow her on Twitter
@ruby_shamir

GILLIAN FLINT has worked as a professional illustrator since earning an animation and illustration degree in 2003. Her work has since been published in the UK, USA and Australia. In her spare time, Gillian enjoys reading, spending time with her family and puttering about in the garden on sunny days. She lives in the northwest of England.

You can visit Gillian Flint online at
gillianflint.com
or follow her on Twitter
@GillianFlint
and on Instagram
@gillianflint_illustration

CHELSEA CLINTON is the author of the #1 *New York Times* bestseller *She Persisted: 13 American Women Who Changed the World*; *She Persisted Around the World: 13 Women Who Changed History*; *She Persisted in Sports: American Olympians Who Changed the Game*; *Don't Let Them Disappear: 12 Endangered Species Across the Globe*; *It's Your World: Get Informed, Get Inspired & Get Going!*; *Start Now!: You Can Make a Difference*; with Hillary Clinton, *Grandma's Gardens* and *Gutsy Women*; and, with Devi Sridhar, *Governing Global Health: Who Runs the World and Why?* She is also the Vice Chair of the Clinton Foundation, where she works on many initiatives, including those that help empower the next generation of leaders. She lives in New York City with her husband, Marc, their children and their dog, Soren.

You can follow Chelsea Clinton on Twitter
@ChelseaClinton
or on Facebook at
facebook.com/chelseaclinton

ALEXANDRA BOIGER has illustrated nearly twenty picture books, including the She Persisted books by Chelsea Clinton; the popular Tallulah series by Marilyn Singer; and the Max and Marla books, which she also wrote. Originally from Munich, Germany, she now lives outside of San Francisco, California, with her husband, Andrea, daughter, Vanessa, and two cats, Luiso and Winter.

Photo credit: *Vanessa Blasich*

You can visit Alexandra Boiger online at
alexandraboiger.com
or follow her on Instagram
@alexandra_boiger

Don't miss the rest of the books in the

She Persisted series!

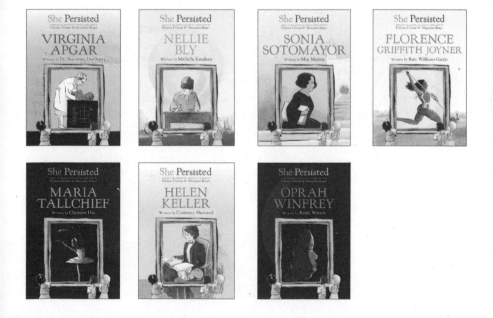